SPECTRUM®
READERS

W9-AYH-403

CREEPY!
Crawlers

By Teresa Domnauer

Carson-Dellosa
Publishing

SPECTRUM

An imprint of Carson-Dellosa Publishing, LLC
P.O. Box 35665
Greensboro, NC 27425-5665

carsondellosa.com

Printed in the USA. All rights reserved.
ISBN 978-1-62399-147-0

01-002131120

You might think a spider is an insect.
You might think a tick is an insect, too.
But they are not!
These creatures belong to
another animal family.
They are arachnids (uh RACK nidz).

Orb Weaver Spider

What does this arachnid do?
It makes strings of silk.
Then, it spins the strings of silk
into a round web.
You might see a spider web like this
in your backyard.

Golden Silk Spider

What does this arachnid do?
It traps insects in its web.
The insects stick to the gooey silk.
They become food for the spider.

8

Wolf Spider

What does this arachnid do?
It hunts for food.
It bites its prey with sharp teeth.
These teeth are called *fangs*.

9

Jumping Spider

What does this arachnid do?
It sneaks up on insects.
Then, it jumps on them and eats them.
The jumping spider also jumps
away from danger.

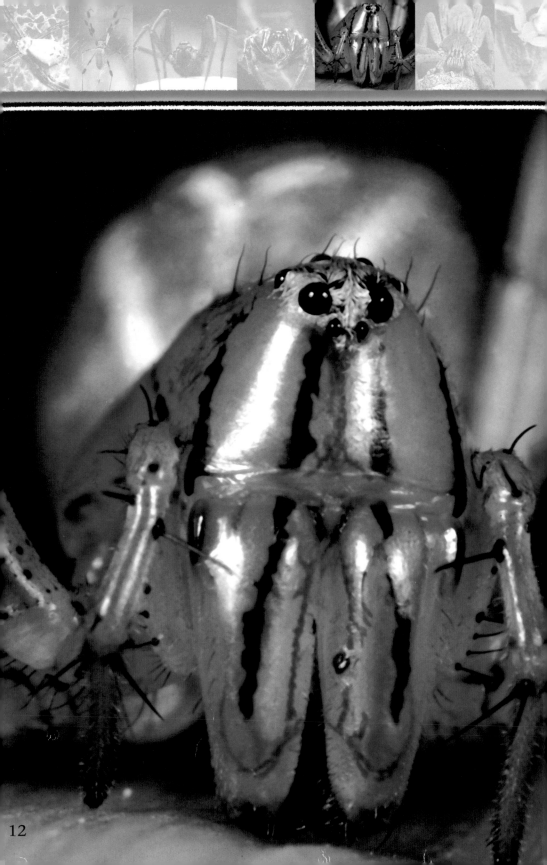

Lynx Spider

What does this arachnid do?
It runs quickly over plants and flowers.
The lynx spider chases insects.
Sometimes, it leaps out and
surprises them.

Huntsman Spider

What does this arachnid do?
It hides in trees.
Its brown color looks like tree bark.
This makes it hard for other animals
to see the huntsman spider.

Crab Spider

What does this arachnid do?
Sometimes, it changes color!
A crab spider hides in flowers.
It can change its color to blend in
with a flower's bright blooms.

Jewel Spider

What does this arachnid do?
It keeps birds away.
Birds do not want to eat
the jewel spider.
It has pointy spines on its body!

Black Widow Spider

What does this arachnid do?
Sometimes, it bites.
Most spiders don't bite people.
But once in a while, the black
widow does.
Its bite can make a person very sick!

Tarantula

What does this arachnid do?
It grows and grows.
Tarantulas are the largest kinds
of spiders in the world.
Some are as big as your hand!

Grass Spider

What does this arachnid do?
It hides in its web.
It waits for an insect to crawl onto it.
Then, it runs quickly to catch it.

26

Daddy Longlegs

What does this arachnid do?
It crawls quickly.
A daddy longlegs has eight
long, thin legs.
It looks a lot like a spider,
but it is a different kind of arachnid.

Scorpion

What does this arachnid do?
It stings.
The scorpion has a sharp stinger
on the end of its tail.
It also has pointy claws
called *pincers* (PIN surz).

Tick

What does this arachnid do?
It crawls onto another animal.
It bites the animal and drinks
its blood.
That is how the tick gets its food!

CREEPY! Crawlers
Comprehension Questions

1. What animal family does a spider belong to?

2. What does an orb weaver spider make?

3. What does a wolf spider use to bite its prey?

4. Do you think a jumping spider uses a web to catch food?

5. What color is the huntsman spider? Why is that color helpful?

6. Why do you think the jewel spider got its name?

7. Which spiders are the largest spiders in the world? How big are these spiders?

8. Is a daddy longlegs a spider?

9. What are a scorpion's pointy claws called?

10. How does a tick get its food?